MATCH of the **DAY**
magazine
ANNUAL 2019

This book belongs to: _I dep store_
Age: _8_
My favourite team is: _Liverpool Under_
My favourite player is: _M Salah_
My highlight of 2018 was: _Qatar_

TOWER HAMLETS
91 D0230196

Welcome!

You can also catch up with MOTD on BBC iPlayer!

Don't forget to keep watching MOTD, readers!

CHEERS, 2018!

HELLO AGAIN! Welcome to the latest instalment of our world-famous Match of the Day Annual. Luckily for you, 2019 is our best yet, featuring the 2018 World Cup, all the biggest stars and loads of funnies and quizzes!

BBC One Don't miss *Match of the Day*, Saturdays and Sundays on BBC One and BBC Two!

IT'S THE QUEEN WITH HER REVIEW OF 2018!

This way, readers!

QUEEN SAYS: "Pippington Guardiola led the City of Manchester to the English crown with a marvellous 100 points – a Premier League record. Jolly good!"

QUEEN SAYS: "The terribly super Mo Salah kicked a record 32 goals – winning him a bejewelled boot and the Professional Footballers' Association award!"

WHO'S ~~NOT~~ INSIDE THIS BOOK...

Ex-British boxing champ Chris Eubank | Loose Women panellist Janet Street-Porter | Dutch darts ace Michael van Gerwen | Tory MP Jacob Rees-Mogg | North Korean leader Kim Jong-Un

CITY OF DREAMS Man. City coasted to the 2017-18 Premier League title!

QUEEN SAYS:
"Chelsea Blues of London out-scored United of Manchester in the Football Association Challenge Cup Trophy finale by one to zero!"

QUEEN SAYS:
"Gareth Bale's splendid upside-down kick and a frightful Loris Karius howler helped Royal Madrid beat Liverpool 3-1 in the League of Champions!"

QUEEN SAYS:
"One sends congratulations to the new world champions France who beat something called Croatia in the Commonwealth Cup final!"

QUEEN SAYS:
"Blessings to a gentleman called Ronald Cristiano, who brought to an end a decade at Royal Madrid to join Italian club Juventus for £100m!"

WHAT'S INSIDE YOUR MOTD ANNUAL?

96 pages of footy fun!

Kylian **MBAPPE**

p6 Bonjour, Monsieur Mbappe

p17 The A-Z of the world's best players

THE EVOLUTION OF **FOOTBALL!**

p26 The evolution of football

p51 The epic tale of the 2018 World Cup

ENGLAND | FRANCE

p65 The big map of Euro footy

p77 Superstars of the past, present & future

Kylian

MBA

A world champion at 19, so what next for Kylian Mbappe?

It's up to him – he runs the game now!

Turn over to read about his **incredible journey so far!**

1998...

Kylian is born on 20 December, five months after France lifted the 1998 World Cup! His dad is from Cameroon and his mum is Algerian, but Kylian grows up 10km outside Paris with his adopted brother Jires, and is soon joined by younger brother Ethan!

IDOLS...

Like most kids of his age, Kylian's heroes are Cristiano Ronaldo and Thierry Henry!

TALENT...

"Kylian could do much more than the other children. His dribbling was already fantastic and he was faster than the others," said his U-13 coach at local club AS Bondy. At 14 he joins Monaco, turning down loads of other Ligue 1 clubs, plus Real Madrid, Chelsea, Man. City, Liverpool and Bayern Munich!

DEBUT...

Two years after arriving in Monaco, Kylian is ready for the first team, and on 2 December 2015 he becomes the club's youngest player ever, aged 16 years, 347 days – beating Thierry Henry's record!

THE BEST YOUNG PLAYER IN THE WORLD!

Kylian went home with the Best Young Player award from Russia 2018. Check out some of the previous winners!

1958 PELE	1962 FLORIAN ALBERT	1966 FRANZ BECKENBAUER	1970 TEOFILO CUBILLAS	1974 WLADYSLAW ZMUDA	1978 ANTONIO CABRINI	1982 MANUEL AMOROS

INTERNATIONAL...

↓ Kylian hits five goals as France win the 2016 Euros at U-19 level. Eight months later, he makes his senior debut in a 3-1 victory over Luxembourg!

EUROPE....

↘ Mbappe's epic performance in Monaco's 6-6 aggregate away goals win over Man. City in the 2016-17 UCL last 16 puts him on the world's radar. He scores twice and is compared to Thierry Henry!

PARIS....

↓ PSG announce they have signed Kylian on loan for 2017-18 with an option to buy him for £166m, making him the second-most expensive player ever. He plays up front with the most expensive (Neymar) and together they score 34 goals and win a treble!

RUSSIA....

↓ Kylian scores from 25 yards to help France beat Croatia 4-2, becoming the first teenager since Pele to score in the World Cup final. He also bags the Best Young Player award and is tipped to take over from Messi and Ronaldo as the world's best baller!

1986	1990	1994	1998	2002	2006	2010	2014
ENZO SCIFO	ROBERT PROSINECKI	MARC OVERMARS	MICHAEL OWEN	LANDON DONOVAN	LUKAS PODOLSKI	THOMAS MULLER	PAUL POGBA

TURN OVER FOR MORE!

SLIDING TOWARDS BALLON D'ORS LIKE....

MBAPPE'S TROPHY CABINET!

A reminder he won all this by the age of 19!

 Ligue 1 x2

 Coupe De France

 Coupe De La Ligue

 World Cup Best Young Player award

 World Cup

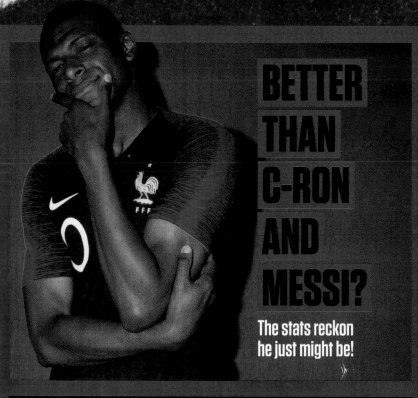

BETTER THAN C-RON AND MESSI?

The stats reckon he just might be!

MBAPPE FIRST THREE SEASONS 2015-18

GAMES **68** GOALS **29** GOALS-PER-GAME RATIO **0.43**

MESSI FIRST THREE SEASONS 2004-07

GAMES **50** GOALS **21** GOALS-PER-GAME RATIO **0.42**

RONALDO FIRST THREE SEASONS 2002-05

GAMES **87** GOALS **12** GOALS-PER-GAME RATIO **0.14**

Kylian's trademark goal celebration was inspired by his little bro Ethan who would celebrate like that when he beat his big bro at FIFA!

MBAPPÉ

Kylian had a trial with Chelsea in 2010 and played against Charlton – but eventually decided to start his career with Monaco!

A move he used to do as a kid that he still does now is the stepover – it was his trademark as a boy. From seven or eight years old he was doing that. He was the best player I've ever seen in 15 years coaching here – no-one has even come close!

ANTONIO RICCARDI, KYLIAN'S JUNIOR COACH AT AS BONDY

KYLIAN MBAPPE'S TEKKERS WHEEL!

His ratings out of 20 on *Football Manager*...

- DRIBBLING 18
- FLAIR 18
- TECHNIQUE 17
- PACE 17
- PENALTY TAKING 15
- VISION 14
- PASSING 13
- FINISHING 14

FM dB
Stats powered by the Football Manager Database

PLAYING STYLE!

- ⚽ Cuts inside from both wings
- ⚽ Gets into opposition area
- ⚽ Curls shots
- ⚽ Tries tricks
- ⚽ Runs with the ball often

Keep up to date with all the European results at bbc.co.uk/sport/football

WHERE YOU FROM, MATE?

Just tell us the country these ballers play for!

HOW DID YOU DO? TURN TO p92 FOR THE ANSWERS!

1

NABIL FEKIR
A Algeria | B France ✓ | C Morocco

2

JOSE GIMENEZ
A Spain | B Colombia | C Uruguay ✓

3

EVER BANEGA
A Argentina ✓ | B Peru | C Chile

4

DANIJEL SUBASIC
A Serbia | B Croatia ✓ | C Russia

5

WILFRED NDIDI
A Nigeria ✓ | B Senegal | C Ghana

6

YOURI TIELEMANS
A Turkey | B Belgium ✓ | C France

7

DAVINSON SANCHEZ
A Colombia ✓ | B Spain | C Peru

8

ANGELO OGBONNA
A Nigeria | B Italy ✓ | C Germany

9

JOEL MATIP
A Cameroon ✓ | B DR Congo | C Mali

THE A-Z

OF THE WORLD'S
BEST PLAYERS!

TURN OVER FOR MORE!

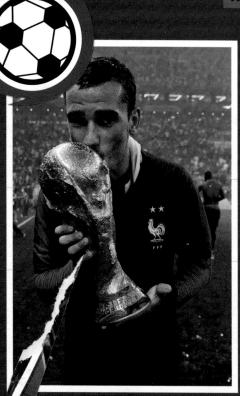

A IS FOR...

ANTOINE GRIEZMANN

It'll be no surprise to learn we're going to start our A to Z with the letter A – and the name that leaps out of our shortlist is Atletico Madrid's World Cup winner Antoine Griezmann. Grizi, who joined Atletico in 2014 from Real Sociedad, would walk into any squad on the planet!

B IS FOR... ## BERNARDO SILVA

He's not even the best Silva at Man. City but there's no-one better with a name beginning with B! The gifted Portugal attacker is only 24 and is capable of conjuring up moments of magic – in a couple of years he could be the star Silva at the Etihad!

C IS FOR... ## CRISTIANO RONALDO

It's still weird seeing the 33-year-old superhero in black and white stripes – but even if he was playing in his pyjamas, he'd be in our alphabet line-up. How could he not be? More than 650 career goals, 25 club trophies, Euro 2016 winner, a record five Ballons d'Or and an insane amount of individual accolades – the Portguese megastar is simply one of the best of all time!

D IS FOR...

DAVID DE GEA

An alien visiting Earth back in June would be scratching their little green head at this decision. DDG had a mare at the World Cup, but he's still the planet's No.1 No.1!

E IS FOR...

EDEN HAZARD

Seven months after Belgium's 1990 World Cup defeat by England, the Belgians were still crying into their waffles. But they shouldn't have been – because in a little town in central Belgium a future genius was being born. Eden Hazard is now a true Red Devils legend!

F IS FOR...

FERNANDINHO

We had three Brazil midfielders in contention for F – Liverpool's Fabinho, Man. United's Fred and Man. City's Fernandinho. Tough call. But for what he's done over the past five seasons, it had to be Ferny!

TURN OVER FOR MORE!

G IS FOR... GARETH BALE

There could only ever be one choice for G! On his day, Bale is unstoppable. Whether that's charging down the wing bashing defenders out of the way, galloping through on goal with just the keeper to beat or flying through the air to execute the most glorious of overhead kicks. The king of Wales is footy royalty!

H IS FOR... HARRY KANE

When Harry finished top scorer in Russia, he made it a hat-trick of Golden Boots – his World Cup award taking pride of place alongside his two Prem Golden Boots from 2015-16 and 2016-17. In short, the Tottenham goal king's scoring record over the past four seasons has been phenomenal!

IS FOR... ISCO

"I think you'll find," said the alphabet official, peering over his spectacles. "That his proper name is Francisco Roman Alarcon Suarez. So he shouldn't be eligible for the letter I." Whatevs, mate. Everyone knows him as Isco. And Isco is the business!

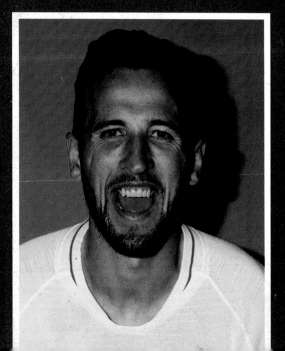

K IS FOR... KYLIAN MBAPPE

Whoever decided we should do an A to Z of the world's best players has stitched us up. On one hand you've got playmaking genius Kevin De Bruyne and on the other Kylian Mbappe. We're a sucker for pace and tricks, so we're going for Kylian!

L IS FOR... LIONEL MESSI

We just feel sorry for every other footballer out there whose name begins with L – Luka Modric, Luis Suarez, Leroy Sane – they just don't stand a chance as long as Leo Messi is lacing up his boots and kicking a ball around!

O IS FOR... OUSMANE DEMBELE

There are more Dembeles in footy than there are penguins in the Antarctic. Ousmane, who Barca paid almost £135.5m for last year, is still only 21 and is set to be the best of the lot!

J IS FOR... JAMES RODRIGUEZ

Yeah, it's pronounced Hamez but it's still a J. The Colombian playmaker has the lot – vision, creativty and can produce moments of goal-scoring brilliance!

M IS FOR... MOHAMED SALAH

Many historians would list the pyramids as Egypt's greatest gift to the world – they obviously haven't seen Mo! The Liverpool forward blitzed his way to the Prem Golden Boot last season – scoring 32 goals in 36 games!

N IS FOR... NEYMAR

Neymar would change the name of Brazil to Neymarland if he could. He'd have us all put up a framed picture of him in our living rooms. And he'd prefer not to be tackled. Ever. But he is awesome!

TURN OVER FOR MORE!

P IS FOR...

PHILIPPE COUTINHO

Another Barca man, another who cost big bucks – £142m, in fact. Phil is one of those players who has his own special move – defenders know it's coming but still can't stop it. He cuts inside from the left and then curls shots from 20 yards with his right foot into the top corner!

Q IS FOR...

QUINCY PROMES

Okay, YOU find someone better whose name starts with Q – it's not easy. For those that don't know, Quincy Promes is a 26-year-old Dutch winger who plays for Sevilla and Holland – and he's not actually that bad!

R IS FOR... ROBERT LEWANDOWSKI

He doesn't strike us as the type of pal who'd give you a big welcoming hug when you pop round for a biscuit – or the sort who'd have a pet bunny rabbit he'd sit and stroke all day. He's ice-cold. He cares not for friends. All Bob Lewandowski cares about is scoring goals – and he does it extremely well!

S IS FOR... SERGIO AGUERO

Shearer, Henry and Kane may raise their eyebrows at the suggestion, but, for some, Kun is the best striker the Prem has ever seen. Kane is the only one with a better strike rate, but Sergio has done it for SEVEN seasons!

T IS FOR... TONI KROOS

Someone please open up Toni Kroos. Undo his exterior casing and locate the laser-guidance device that's inside. There's no other explanation for the accuracy of his passing, over all distances and probably all terrains. The Real Madrid midfielder must be a robot in disguise – and we want proof!

U IS FOR... UROS SPAJIC

He's not a household name, but like with the letter Q, there aren't a lot of players out there whose name starts with U – and Uros Spajic is the best of the lot. The 25-year-old centre-back was part of Serbia's World Cup squad!

V IS FOR... VINCENT KOMPANY

The Belgian is now in his 11th season at Man. City – and what an 11 seasons they've been. Not only has he won eight trophies and been named in multiple PFA Team of the Year, he's been an inspirational leader!

W IS FOR... WILLIAN

He's a manager's dream. He's got the talent, he's got the quick feet, the acceleration, the touch and the tricks – but he's also got the stamina, the energy and the desire to work hard. He'll track back, he won't stop running and that's why managers love him!

X IS FOR... XHERDAN SHAQIRI

Between 2006 and 2015, X was always Xavi. The king of the tiki-taka was a genius. But he's now slouching around in the Qatari league, so there's only one X-man for the job – Liverpool's Swiss winger Xherdan Shaqiri!

Y IS FOR... YOURI TIELEMANS

When we asked our scout to compile a list of Y stars, he came up with Colombia centre-back Yerry Mina, RB Leipzig forward Yussuf Poulsen and Belgium winger Yannick Carrasco. But we reckon 21-year-old Monaco and Belgium ace Youri is gonna be the star!

Z IS FOR... ZLATAN IBRAHIMOVIC

What a way to end our alphabet of all-stars – with the one and only Zlatan. Along with the meatball and Ikea, this man is the greatest Swedish export of all time. Since making his debut in 1999, Ibra has won 12 titles in four different countries. Legend!

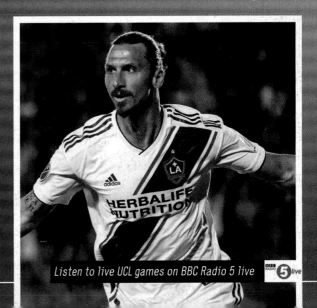

Listen to live UCL games on BBC Radio 5 live

A YEAR IN FOOTBALL!

How much can you remember about 2018? Let's find out...

HOW DID YOU DO? TURN TO p92 FOR THE ANSWERS!

1

Who finished runners-up to Man. City in the Prem last season?

A	Man. United	✓
B	Tottenham	
C	Liverpool	

2

What was the score in the FA Cup final?

A	Chelsea 1-0 Man. United	✓
B	Chelsea 2-0 Man. United	
C	Chelsea 2-1 Man. United	✓

3

Which English team went furthest in the UCL last season?

A	Man. City	
B	Tottenham	
C	Liverpool	✓

4

Who won the Premier League Golden Boot?

A	Harry Kane	✓
B	Romelu Lukaku	
C	Mohamed Salah	✓

5

Who was top scorer in La Liga last season?

A	Lionel Messi	✓
B	Luis Suarez	
C	Cristiano Ronaldo	

6

Which Chelsea player made the 2017-18 PFA Team of the Year?

A	N'Golo Kante	✓
B	Eden Hazard	
C	Marcos Alonso	

7

Arsenal boss Unai Emery also managed which club in 2018?

A	Monaco	
B	PSG	✓
C	Valencia	

8

Naby Keita joined Liverpool from which Bundesliga club?

A	Bayer Leverkusen	
B	RB Leipzig	✓
C	Borussia Dortmund	✓

9

Who was sacked as manager of Stoke in January 2018?

A	Mark Hughes	✓
B	Paul Lambert	
C	Tony Pulis	

How to be

YOUR HERO!

Cut out & keep your fave posters!

Five players, one amazing guide to how **YOU** can be exactly like your favourite footballer!

The style of play! The signature move! The hair! The shirt number! The car! The boots! The motto!

TURN OVER FOR MORE!

LIONEL MESSI

Full name Lionel Andres Messi Cuccittini
Age 31 **Club** Barcelona
Country Argentina
Height 5ft 7in
Best attribute Dribbling

MOTTO
"The best decisions aren't made with your mind, but with your instinct!"

STYLE OF PLAY
It's not easy playing like Leo, but a good start is finding space in attacking areas, keeping the ball and being clinical in front of goal!

SIGNATURE MOVE
Burn down the right wing, cut inside, take on two players, play a one-two, take a touch and whip into the top corner with your left foot!

HAIR
He's had long hair, short hair and dyed blond hair, but right now Leo is keeping it simple. Ask for a faded side sweep!

SHIRT NUMBER
Only real ballers can rock the No.10 – you've got to be a creative force!

CAR
Messi has a fleet of fast cars worth £2.7m, but loves zipping about in his Mini Cooper!

BOOTS
Leo wears his own version of Adidas Nemeziz. They're so lightweight it feels like you're barefoot!
£89.95 adidas.co.uk

How to be like...
CRISTIANO RONALDO

A born winner who looks the part, leads from the front and never buckles under pressure!

Full name Cristiano Ronaldo Dos Santos Aveiro **Age** 33 **Club** Juventus **Country** Portugal **Height** 6ft 1in **Best attribute** Finishing

MOTTO
"Talent without working hard is nothing!"

STYLE OF PLAY
Ronaldo is all about motivating his team-mates, hard work and being clinical in the big moments. Be ready to pounce in the penalty area!

SIGNATURE MOVE
When the whistle blows and the ref points to the spot, C-Ron always steps up and delivers. Get yourself on pens and free-kicks!

HAIR
It's hard to keep up with his cuts, but his latest is super-short on the sides and slick on top. The message? Be brave!

SHIRT NUMBER
The No.7 used to be for assist kings, but C-Ron's made it all about goals!

CAR
CR7's garage is packed with supercars, one of which is the latest Ferrari F12!

BOOTS
Just like Leo, Ronaldo balls in his own Nike Mercurials that lock in around the ankle with a collar! **£155** prodirectsoccer.com

TURN OVER FOR MORE!

How to be like...
NEYMAR

PSG's samba star is a skilful, speedy tekkers machine who always plays with a smile on his face!

Full name Neymar Da Silva Santos Junior **Age** 26 **Club** PSG **Country** Brazil **Height** 5ft 9in **Best attribute** Skills

MOTTO
"The secret is to believe in your dreams and your potential to be like your hero!"

STYLE OF PLAY
Some players get nervous in tight situations and give the ball away. Not Ney – he busts out his tekkers and kills it. Express yourself!

SIGNATURE MOVE
While dribbling at pace, drag the ball across your body, then perform a stepover with the other foot and flick it past the defender!

HAIR
His curly style isn't for everyone, but looks sick when done right. Ask for a few highlights if you want the full look!

SHIRT NUMBER
Bag that No.10 jersey and tell your gaffer you're ready to be the star man!

CAR
Ferraris, Maseratis and Audis sit on Neymar's drive, but he's also got a Volkswagen Touareg!

BOOTS
Ney's Vapors with Nike's All Conditions Control tech will keep your control on point! £120 prodirectsoccer.com

How to be like...
PAUL POGBA

France's dab-loving midfielder entertains football fans on and off the pitch with his style!

Full name Paul Labile Pogba **Age** 25 **Club** Man. United **Country** France **Height** 6ft 3in **Best attribute** Stamina

MOTTO
"If you feel something, just do it!"

STYLE OF PLAY
Pop off long shots, link the midfield to attack and don't be afraid of getting stuck in – and throw in the odd stepover now and then!

SIGNATURE MOVE
Apart from his sidewinder cross-field balls, his main move has got to be the dab, so don't forget to hit it when you score!

HAIR
The key is not to be afraid of trying something. Red mohawks, blue lines or shaved off – just make it your own!

SHIRT NUMBER
The No.6 comes with responsibility – you need to pull the strings in midfield!

CAR
Work hard and you never know, you too might have a £250,000 Rolls Royce like Pogba!

BOOTS
Pog bosses the midfield in his classic red-and-black pair of Adidas Predators. **£119.95** adidas.co.uk

TURN OVER FOR MORE!

How to be like...
PIERRE-EMERICK AUBAMEYANG

Speedy feet, sweet personalised boots and a mohawk – Auba is always on flames!

Full name Pierre-Emerick Emiliano Francois Aubameyang **Age** 29 **Club** Arsenal **Country** Gabon **Height** 6ft 2in **Best attribute** Acceleration

MOTTO
"I always set myself goals. I always want to do better than I did in the past!"

STYLE OF PLAY
Everything Pierre does is at pace – his movement, his passing and his pressing. So get your skates on and zip around!

SIGNATURE MOVE
A clinical finish followed by a somersault, although you shouldn't try the cele without advice from a professional gymnast first!

HAIR
Keep it faded on the sides and long on top. Then, push it up into the centre until it all meets to create the Auba spike!

SHIRT NUMBER
No.14 seem like a sub's shirt, but Auba has made it cool and you can, too!

CAR
The Gabon striker loves to roll around London in his sick Lamborghini Aventador!

BOOTS
Pierre is all about the limited-edition wheels, so get on Nike ID and design your own pair!
nikeid.com

OLD GAME!

⚽ Pep's canal calamity! Otamendi is throwing more than just shade!

Otamendi's been arrested for throwing something in the canal, sir!

Oh no! What did he throw?

Pep gets an urgent message from his security staff...

Stones, sir!

Stones? Hardly an offence is it?

It was John Stones, sir!

⚽ Top of the stupidity table! Mesut has had a mare there!

I wish I'd brought the kitchen table!

Huh?

In the Arsenal dressing room pre-match...

Why would you bring your kitchen table to the football?

Because I left my shinpads on it!

⚽ Klopp's sketchy tactics! The art of management isn't easy!

Jurgen Klopp is not happy...

Why aren't you ready? The match is about to start!

You said you wanted us to draw the match today!

So, that's what we're doing, boss – drawing!

You imbeciles!

THE BIG 5!

How do the Prem's superclubs compare to each other?

CLUB	FOUNDED	STADIUM	TROPHIES WON	LEAGUE TITLES
Arsenal	1886	Emirates Stadium 59,867	46	13
Chelsea	1905	Stamford Bridge 41,631	30	6
Liverpool	1892	Anfield 54,074	61	18
Manchester City	1880	Etihad Stadium 55,097	20	5
Manchester United	1878	Old Trafford 74,994	66	20

Premier League

PAZ SAYS
Man. United are the biggest Prem club in terms of finance, fanbase and trophies won!

UCL WINNERS	RECORD SIGNING	MOST APPEARANCES	RECORD SCORER	2018-19 SEASON
0	**PIERRE-EMERICK AUBAMEYANG** £56m from B. Dortmund, 2018	**DAVID O'LEARY** 722 GAMES 1975-93	**THIERRY HENRY** 228 GOALS 1999-2007 & 2012	Manager: Unai Emery Captain: Laurent Koscielny Star player: P.E. Aubameyang
1	**KEPA ARRIZABALAGA** £71.6m from Athletic Bilbao, 2018	**RON HARRIS** 795 GAMES 1961-80	**FRANK LAMPARD** 211 GOALS 2001-14	Manager: Maurizio Sarri Captain: Gary Cahill Star player: Eden Hazard
5	**VIRGIL VAN DIJK** £75m from Southampton, 2018	**IAN CALLAGHAN** 857 GAMES 1960-78	**IAN RUSH** 346 GOALS 1980-87 & 1988-96	Manager: Jurgen Klopp Captain: Jordan Henderson Star player: Mo Salah
0	**RIYAD MAHREZ** £60m from Leicester, 2018	**ALAN OAKES** 676 GAMES 1959-76	**SERGIO AGUERO** 204 GOALS 2011-	Manager: Pep Guardiola Captain: Vincent Kompany Star player: Kevin De Bruyne
3	**PAUL POGBA** £89m from Juventus, 2016	**RYAN GIGGS** 963 GAMES 1991-2014	**WAYNE ROONEY** 253 GOALS 2004-17	Manager: Jose Mourinho Captain: Antonio Valencia Star player: David De Gea

All stats correct up to 4 September 2018

Watch Prem highlights on MOTD, Saturday evenings, on BBC One

BBC one

CAPTAIN!

SILENT SPARK!

WHAT TYPE OF

HEADLINE MAKER!

JOKER!

VERSATILE GEM!

BALLER ARE YOU?

There are loads of different tekkers kings out there, but which best describes you? Tick each explanation that applies to your game and find out what you are!

TURN OVER FOR MORE!

There is a ruck in the box, the ref is having to pull opposition players apart – so what do you do? Drag your team-mates away and calm them down, of course!

Nothing gives you more pleasure on a football pitch than intercepting a dangerous through-ball – not even scoring a goal!

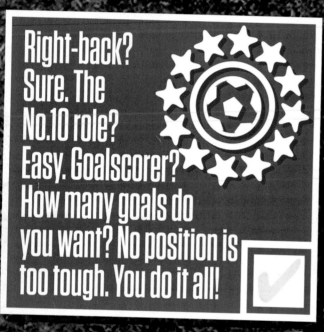

Right-back? Sure. The No.10 role? Easy. Goalscorer? How many goals do you want? No position is too tough. You do it all!

It's five minutes to kick-off. The nerves are setting in around the changing room. You stand up and remind the group what their jobs are and get the atmosphere pumping!

Your team has won a penalty. You sprint into to box and grab the ball!

There's an injury break. Time to get some water, right? Wrong. Perfect time to eye up the ice cream van menu for full-time!

The manager puts you on all set-pieces – free-kicks, corners, penalties and sometimes even goal kicks!

When your team-mate asks how long till the full-time whistle goes, you're wondering whether that's enough time to hit the top bins again!

You regularly pick up the man of the match award, but just put it straight into your bag and start focusing on the next game!

Ooh, look at that – a cute little doggy riding a skateboard!

Oh no! Your left-back has just given away a penalty in the dying seconds. You could scream at them, but no – you put your arm round them and tell them to come back stronger!

When your right-back has charged forward, leaving a gap in the defence, you know to slot in until they're back!

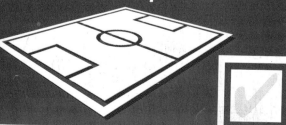

TURN OVER FOR MORE!

Your batteries never run out. You could run all day if need be. Playing football is just great fun to you! ✔

Rain, hail or blistering sun – whatever the weather, it never affects your game. You can play in all conditions! ✔

You run the changing room – from picking the pre-match tunes to playing the funniest pranks! ✔

Your voice is heard everywhere during a match, organising your team, encouragi them and motivating ✔

"Winners never quit and quitters never win" is your motto. Even when there are seconds to go, you still believe there's a chance for glory! ✔

Half-time is a great opportunity to trade Match Attax cards! Well, when else am I going to do it?

Black boots are for referees – you only wear the brightest, sickest boots on the market!

The last time you missed a training session was when it got snowed off in winter. You're always there, no matter what!

WHAT TYPE OF BALLER ARE YOU?

Add up all the boxes you ticked, see what colour you marked the most and find out what type of player you are!

MOSTLY RED	MOSTLY BLUE	MOSTLY GREEN	MOSTLY YELLOW	MOSTLY PURPLE

CAPTAIN, LEADER, LEGEND!

Nothing makes you prouder than pulling on that strip and leading your team out to fight for the three points. You set the standard and are the player your team-mates look up to. Football is more than just a game to you!

SILENT SPARK!

Chasing, dribbling and stealing the ball off the opposition is easy work for you. You're always at training, putting in the hard yards and regularly pick up the MOTM award – but you never brag. Every team needs someone like you!

THE HEADLINE MAKER!

Just when your team-mates are starting to sink under pressure, you drag them out of the mud with something special. Your locker is bursting with sidewinders, scorpion kicks and top-bins knuckleballs!

VERSATILE GEM!

You can play in multiple positions to a high standard. You're comfortable with both feet, on all set-pieces and consistently put in 7 out of 10 displays. You might not realise it, but you're one of your gaffer's most important players, Mr Reliable!

THE JOKER!

Let's face it – you love footy, but you're not the best. You turn up to have banter with mates, love the pre-match sleepovers and get a 99 at the full-time whistle. You'd secretly prefer to get left out of the squad so you can open FUT packs!

Check out the latest transfer rumours at bbc.co.uk/sport/football/gossip **gossip**

MAN. CITY
PREMIER LEAGUE CHAMPIONS

2017-18 LEAGUE

JUVENTUS
SERIE A CHAMPIONS

PSG
LIGUE 1 CHAMPIONS

WINNERS!

BAYERN MUNICH
BUNDESLIGA CHAMPIONS

DEUTSCHER FUSSBALLMEISTER 2018

FC BAYERN MÜNCHEN

BARCELONA
LA LIGA CHAMPIONS

CELTIC
SCOTTISH PREM CHAMPIONS

MATCH of the **DAY** magazine

NEYMAR
Illustrator: Tom Griffiths
tomgriffiths.online

Cut out & keep your fave posters!

Seleção

VIVE LA FRANCE!

Are there any sweets inside this thing?

FROM RUSSIA WITH LOLS!

15 wonderful World Cup stories

TURN OVER FOR MORE!

HOODOO

FLIPPIN' 'ECK!

His palms are sweaty, knees weak, arms are heavy,
All eyes are on Iran's Milad Mohammadi!

He's nervous, his country need a goal with seconds to go,
So Milad tries a forward roll long throw!

You're jokin', now? Everybody's chokin', ha!
The clocks run out, times up, Iran are out!

HEADS UP!

Fetch the memes, make the GIFs,
Michy's come a cropper!

Belgium have scored
and Batman wellied it proper!

But into the net the ball did not fly,
No, it came back off the post,
And into his eye!

Ooh, me
poor bonce
is all hurty!

HEAVEN!

The hoodoo, the curse, it's finally gone,
England faced pens and finally won!

Q

This was for Waddle, for Batty, for Southgate,
Pickford's top hand, then Dier – it's fate!

Q

Time for a pile on, red bodies galore,
Oh, how we enjoyed The Three Lions roar!

OH DEAR, DEUTSCHLAND!

No way, you're kidding, this cannot be true,
This is Germany, man – they always go through!

Q

Not this time, my friend – look at those tears,
They've been dumped out by the cheeky South Koreans!

Q

Auf wiedersehen, lads, cheerio, ta-ta,
The Germans are out – don't mention the VAR!

NIGERIA'S THREADS!

The body was green, the shoulders were black,
Nigeria's kit was a lovely throwback!

Q

We'll never forget those zig-zags so bold,
Apparently, Nike said, there were three million sold!

TURN OVER FOR MORE!

RONALDO NIGHT!

HISTORY

Portugal's opener wasn't the easiest game,
The European champions had to play Spain!

With two minutes left they needed a goal,
And Cristiano Ronaldo stood over the ball!

He took a deep breath and bypassed the wall,
Portugal were level thanks to Ron's three-goal haul!

14 MINUTES!

He dived and he rolled,
He moaned and he whined,
Neymar's World Cup can be summed up by time!

He spent 14 minutes on the Russian floor,
Any longer and Ney would have started to snore!

BOY!

OUT WITH THE OLD!

Don't pinch yourself, Kylian – this isn't a dream,
You're one of the best the world's ever seen!

〰

You scored one in the final, this is your day,
The last to do that was a certain Pele!

〰

The crowd's jaws were dropped, you left them in awe,
It's a matter of time before you win a Ballon d'Or!

They came to conquer but crashed and burned,
For Ronaldo and Messi it was a final chance spurned!

〰

The World Cup trophy remains out of their reach,
But their talent and skills you simply can't teach!

〰

Is one better than the other, it's not possible to say,
It was fitting their dreams ended on the very same day!

Can I call you back, Mum? Just gotta check the VAR!

VAR-Y GOOD!

Well done VAR you've made us all hypocrites,
Video refs rock, even in their full kits!

〰

We thought you'd be rubbish and slow down the games,
But instead you help settle tight penalty claims!

〰

It brought nail-biting moments and won England two pens,
Okay, it's not perfect, we'll give it an 8 out of 10!

TURN OVER FOR MORE!

GOLDEN BOOT BOY!

THE RUSSIAN REVELATION!

Worst Russian team ever, they'll not win a game,
Some so-called experts made embarrassing claims!

The Russians found form on the world's biggest stage,
The country went wild when Aspas' pen was saved!

They inspired the nation and proved doubters wrong,
In the hearts of a nation these players belong!

WAISTCOAT DREAMS!

It's a sleeveless garment, worn over a shirt,
But it came close to ending 52 years of hurt!

Gareth's waistcoat was slick, he pulled it off with ease,
Watching him wear it made us really believe!

In the end England lost, football didn't come home,
This man should be knighted, get the Queen on the phone!

I was gonna wear me onesie, MOTD!

The favourites were Messi, Ronaldo and Grizi,
But Harry made winning it look pretty easy!

A header, some pens, even one off his heel,
Taking home the Golden Boot is a pretty big deal!

The last English winner is certain presenter,
Harry and Gary, top defence tormentors!

PICKERS' MAGIC BOTTLE!

Did you hear about Pickford's secret penalty tracker,
He used it to save from Colombia's Bacca!

On his bottle, he scribbled where pen-takers might hit,
Thank goodness Colombia's keeper didn't take a sip!

RELEASE THE SWAZ!

Oh, what a hit, Nacho pretty much broke the net,
Goal of the Tournament seemed a pretty safe bet!

But here's Quaresma with the outside of his boot,
The shape on his shot made even Ronaldo salute!

Yet the swaz being copied in everyone's backyard,
Belongs to French right-back Benjamin Pavard!

MATCH of the DAY magazine

HARRY KANE
Illustrator: Stanley Chow
stanleychow.co.uk

Cut out & keep your fave posters!

Is your brain ready for this challenge?

FAMILY FOOTY
QUIZ TIME!

Grab your mum, dad, big brother, sister or your pet hamster and sit down together to crack this bumper footy quiz!

TURN OVER FOR MORE!

ENGLISH FOOTBALL!

1 Which of these clubs has never won the FA Cup?

A Crystal Palace ✓   B Cardiff ✓   C Huddersfield ✓   D Sunderland ✓

2 Which of these stars has NOT been PFA Player of the Year?

A Harry Kane ✓   B Riyad Mahrez ✓

C N'Golo Kante ✓   D Eden Hazard ✓

3 Which Championship club play their games at Ashton Gate?

A Norwich ✓   B Rotherham ✓
C Bristol City ✓   D Preston ✓

4 Which Prem team did this man manage in 2007-08 season?

A Tottenham ✓   B Chelsea ✓
C West Ham ✓   D Newcastle ✓

5 Which player has made the most Prem appearances?

A Theo Walcott ✓   B Aaron Lennon ✓

C David Silva ✓   D Mark Noble ✓

6 Which of these Football League clubs is known as The Grecians?

A Stevenage ☑   B Grimsby ☑   C Exeter ☑   D Lincoln ☑

7 Can you name this 2009-10 Premier League winner?

A Miroslav Stoch
B Fabio Borini
C Branislav Ivanovic
D Ben Sahar

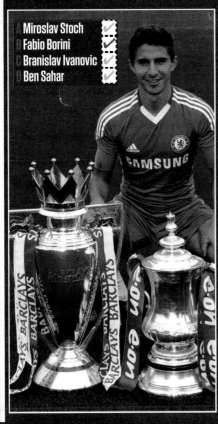

8 Which of these clubs has Kyle Walker not played for?

A Sheff. United ☑   B Aston Villa ☑
C QPR ☑   D Barnsley ☑

9 Which of these Man. United players is the oldest?

A Juan Mata ☑   B Marouane Fellaini ☑

C Nemanja Matic ☑   D Alexis Sanchez ☑

10 Which of these players has scored in an FA Cup final?

A Laurent Koscielny ☑   B Sergio Aguero ☑   C Jordan Henderson ☑   D Yannick Bolasie ☑

TURN OVER FOR MORE!

REST OF THE WORLD!

11

Which of these clubs has never won Spain's La Liga?

A Sevilla ☑ | B Real Betis ☑ | C Real Sociedad ☑ | D Celta Vigo ☑

---

12 ### Which of these is Croatian star Ivan Perisic?

A ☑ | B ☑

C ☑ | D ☑

---

13 ### Which European superclub play at this epic stadium?

A Juventus ☑ | B Bayern Munich ☑
C Real Madrid ☑ | D Porto ☑

---

14 ### What country does Juventus' Miralem Pjanic play for?

A Serbia ☑ | B Bosnia & Herzegovina ☑
C Croatia ☑ | D Albania ☑

---

15 ### Which of these players has never scored in a UCL final?

A Alvaro Morata ☑ | B R. Lewandowski ☑

C Ilkay Gundogan ☑ | D Diego Godin ☑

---

16 Which of these clubs doesn't play in Argentina?

A Boca Juniors ☑

B River Plate ☑

C Gremio ☑

D Velez Sarsfield ☑

17 In which country does Andres Iniesta now play his football?

A China ☑
B Japan ☑
C UAE ☑
D Qatar ☑

18 Jonas was top scorer in which country in 2017-18?

A Turkey ☑
B Belgium ☑
C Portugal ☑
D Brazil ☑

19 Who has been Europe's top scorer on the most occasions?

A Lionel Messi ☑

B Cristiano Ronaldo ☑

C Marco van Basten ☑

D Gerd Muller ☑

20 Which of these is Galatasaray keeper Fernando Muslera?

A ☑

B ☑

C ☑

D ☑

HOW DID YOU DO?

TURN TO p92 FOR THE ANSWERS!

Watch Prem highlights on MOTD, Saturday evenings, on BBC One BBC one

MATCH of the DAY magazine
CRISTIANO RONALDO
Illustrator: Mark Johnson
markjohnsondesign.co.uk

Cut out & keep your fave posters!

MOTD mag brings you key facts about Europe's five biggest footy nations!

THE ULTIMATE GUIDE TO EUROPEAN FOOTBALL!

TURN OVER FOR MORE!

NEWCASTLE

LEEDS

MANCHESTER

LIVERPOOL

SHEFFIELD

Hello!

BIRMINGHAM

LONDON

FACT FILE!
Population: 55 million
Area: 130,279km²
Capital: London
Currency: Pound Sterling £
Prime Minister: Theresa May

+ ENGLAND

Governing body The Football Association
Founded 1863
Top league Premier League
Major cup comps FA Cup, EFL Cup

BIGGEST STADIUM
WEMBLEY
England national
team, 90,000

THE 2017-18 SEASON
Champions: Man. City Top scorer: Mo Salah, Liverpool, 32 goals
Player of the Year: Mo Salah, Liverpool
Prem average attendance: 38,274 FA Cup winners: Chelsea

MOST TITLES
Man. United 20

TRADITIONAL FOOTBALL STYLE
Fast, physical and direct

TYPICAL HALF-TIME SNACK
Meat pie and Bovril

FACT FILE!
Population **67 million**
Area **640,679km²**
Capital **Paris**
Currency **Euro €**
President **Emmanuel Macron**

PARIS

NANTES

LYON

BORDEAUX

Bonjour!

NICE

MARSEILLE

FRANCE

Governing body **French Football Federation**
Founded **1919** Top league **Ligue 1**
Major cup comps **Coupe De France,
Coupe De La Ligue**

THE 2017-18 SEASON

Champions: **PSG** Top scorer: **Edinson Cavani, PSG, 28 goals**
Player of the Year: **Neymar, PSG** Ligue 1 average attendance: **22,585**
Coupe De France winners: **PSG**

**BIGGEST STADIUM
STADE DE FRANCE**
France national team
81,338

MOST TITLES
Saint-Etienne

TRADITIONAL FOOTBALL STYLE
Style, strength and skill

TYPICAL HALF-TIME SNACK
Galette-saucisse – fried
sausage wrapped in a pancake

TURN OVER FOR MORE!

Guten tag!

FACT FILE!
Population: 83 million
Area: 357,386km²
Capital: Berlin
Currency: Euro €
Chancellor: Angela Merkel

HAMBURG

BERLIN

COLOGNE

FRANKFURT

STUTTGART

MUNICH

GERMANY

Governing body German Football Association
Founded 1900
Top league Bundesliga
Major cup comp DFB-Pokal

BIGGEST STADIUM
SIGNAL IDUNA PARK
Borussia Dortmund
81,359

THE 2017-18 SEASON
Champions: Bayern Munich Top scorer: Robert Lewandowski, Bayern Munich, 29 goals Player of the Year: Naldo, Schalke Bundesliga average attendance: 44,651 DFB-Pokal winners: Eintracht Frankfurt

MOST TITLES
Bayern Munich 27

TRADITIONAL FOOTBALL STYLE
Cool, calm and composed

TYPICAL HALF-TIME SNACK
Bratwurst – a type
of German sausage

MILAN

TURIN

VENICE

FLORENCE

ROME

NAPLES

Ciao!

FACT FILE!

Population: 60 million
Area: 301,340km²
Capital: Rome
Currency: Euro €
Prime minister: Giuseppe Conte

ITALY

Governing body Italian Football Federation
Founded 1898
Top league Serie A
Major cup comp Coppa Italia

ITALIA
FIGC

BIGGEST STADIUM
SAN SIRO
AC Milan & Inter Milan
80,018

THE 2017-18 SEASON

Champions: Juventus Top scorer: Mauro Icardi, Inter Milan, & Ciro Immobile, Lazio, 29 goals
Player of the Year: Gianluigi Buffon, Juventus
Serie A average attendance: 24,738 Coppa Italia winners: Juventus

JUVENTUS

MOST TITLES
Juventus 34

TRADITIONAL FOOTBALL STYLE
Tactical, defensive and clinical

TYPICAL HALF-TIME SNACK
Salamella (Italian sausage) sandwich with onions and paprika

TURN OVER FOR MORE!

BILBAO

BARCELONA

MADRID

VALENCIA

SEVILLE

Hola!

MALAGA

FACT FILE!
Population: 47 million
Area: 505,990km²
Capital: Madrid
Currency: Euro €
Prime minister: Pedro Sanchez

SPAIN

Governing body Royal Spanish Football Association
Founded 1909
Top league La Liga
Major cup comps Copa Del Rey

BIGGEST STADIUM
NOU CAMP
Barcelona
99,354

THE 2017-18 SEASON
Champions: Barcelona Top scorer: Lionel Messi,
Barcelona, 34 goals Player of the Year: Lionel Messi, Barcelona
Average attendance: 26,968 Copa Del Rey winners: Barcelona

MOST TITLES
Real Madrid 33

TRADITIONAL FOOTBALL STYLE
Tiki-Taka – short, one-touch passing

TYPICAL HALF-TIME SNACK
Sunflower seeds

Keep up to date with all the Euro footy action on bbc.co.uk/sport/football

MATCH of the DAY magazine
MARCUS RASHFORD
Illustrator: John Sheehan
john-sportraits.com

✂ Cut out & keep your fave posters!

TOP 8 WOMEN BALLERS!

Say hello to the most lethal ladies in world football right now!

Renard has been France captain since 2013!

8

WENDIE RENARD

CLUB LYON COUNTRY FRANCE POSITION DEFENDER AGE 28

She's won 11 French titles, the Champions League four times and captains her club and country, but it's her record in front of goal that stands out – 19 for France and 67 for Lyon. Not too shabby for a centre-back!

7

VIVIANNE MIEDEMA

CLUB ARSENAL COUNTRY HOLLAND POSITION FORWARD AGE 22

The ex-Bayern Munich star was a big fan of Robin van Persie, which is why she followed in his footsteps and joined The Gunners in 2017. As a flying winger who loves to cut in, Viv models her game on Arjen Robben!

5

PERNILLE HARDER

CLUB WOLFSBURG COUNTRY DENMARK POSITION STRIKER AGE 25

Denmark's captain has won her country's Player of the Year award every year since 2015 for her sick performances in front of goal – her 53 goals in 101 games in red and white have made her a legend in her home nation!

LUCY BRONZE

CLUB LYON COUNTRY ENGLAND POSITION DEFENDER/MIDFIELDER AGE 26

The 2018 BBC's Women's Player of the Year started at Sunderland before moving to America to study. Now, England's versatile gem plays for Europe's best team and once went a whole season unbeaten with Man. City!

6

DZSENIFER
MAROZSAN

CLUB LYON **COUNTRY** GERMANY **POSITION** MIDFIELDER **AGE** 26

Her name is a mouthful, but her trophy haul speaks for itself – 12 titles for club and country, including an Olympic gold, and 14 individual awards make Germany's skipper one of the most-decorated players ever!

4

2

DEYNA
CASTELLANOS

CLUB SANTA CLARITA BLUE HEAT
COUNTRY VENEZUELA **POSITION** FORWARD **AGE** 19

Given that she's never played for a major club, people were surprised to see Deyna in The Best's 2017 top three – but the smart, gifted forward is the rising star of women's footy!

3

CARLI LLOYD

CLUB SKY BLUE **COUNTRY** USA **POSITION** MIDFIELDER **AGE** 36

Carli Lloyd is more than just a footballer – she's a legend! The midfielder has played over 250 times for her country, scored 100 goals, won countless awards and is known for her energy, drive and long-range strikes!

LIEKE
MARTENS

CLUB BARCELONA **COUNTRY** HOLLAND **POSITION** FORWARD **AGE** 25

What a year it's been for the Holland forward – she won the Golden Ball at Euro 2017, FIFA's The Best award and joined Barca! We're not surprised – Lieke bags goals everywhere she goes. She's the Leo Messi of women's football!

Martens is the current FIFA and UEFA Player of the Year!

PAZ SAYS
Lieke has got the lot – she's quick, skilful and is a total match-winner!

1

STADIUM NAME GAME!

Just tell us which stadium the Football League clubs below play at – simple!

HOW DID YOU DO? TURN TO p92 FOR THE ANSWERS!

1

A Carrow Road ✓
B Portman Road ✓
C Blundell Park ✓

2

A The Den ✓
B Brisbane Road ✓
C Griffin Park ✓

3

A Ewood Park ☐
B Ashton Gate ☐
C Pride Park ☐

4

A Riverside Stadium ☐
B Ayresome Park ☐
C City Ground ☐

5

A DW Stadium ☐
B Deepdale ☐
C Bramall Lane ☐

6

A Madejski Stadium ☐
B St Andrew's ☐
C Loftus Road ☐

7

A Glanford Park ☐
B Home Park ☐
C Sixfields Stadium ☐

8

A Valley Parade ☐
B The Valley ☐
C Boundary Park ☐

9

A Bloomfield Road ☐
B Gigg Lane ☐
C Fratton Park ☐

READER OFFER

NEVER MISS AN ISSUE OF

MATCH of the DAY
magazine

OFFER DEADLINE DATE
31 JULY 2019

◆ PAY ONLY £4 for your first 4 issues!

◆ CONTINUE TO SAVE 21%* after your trial!

◆ DELIVERY DIRECT TO YOUR DOOR every week!

◆ NEVER MISS AN ISSUE of your favourite footy mag!

VISIT buysubscriptions.com/MDPANN18

CALL 03330 162 126† QUOTE MDPANN18

Closing date: 31 July 2019. Offer is only available for delivery to UK addresses and for UK Direct Debit customers. You will pay £24.99 every three months but you may cancel at any time.
*The basic annual rate of Match of the Day is £117 per annum. Prices are discounted from the basic annual rate and include P&P. Subject to availability. †UK calls will cost the same as other standard fixed line numbers (starting 01 or 02) and are included in inclusive or free minutes allowances. Outside of free call packages, calls from mobile phones will cost between 3p and 55p per minute. Lines are open 8am-8pm weekdays and 9am-1pm Saturday.

SUPERSTARS

OF THE

PAST, PRESENT

AND

FUTURE!

EVERY PREM CLUB!

We reveal the men who have written or who will be writing their name in your club's history books...

CLUB LEGENDS ☑ HEROES ☑ WONDERKIDS ☑

TURN OVER FOR MORE!

ARSENAL

LEGEND

Thierry Henry
1999–2007 & 2012
Technically superb, explosive French striker who is The Gunners' all-time record goalscorer and a Prem ledge!

SUPER STAR

Pierre-Emerick Aubameyang 2018-
Lightning-quick and razor-sharp Gabon striker who signed from Borussia Dortmund for £56m!

WONDER KID

Emile Smith Rowe Age: 18
Stylish attacking midfielder who can unlock defences and score worldies!

BOURNEMOUTH

LEGEND

Ted MacDougall
1969–72 & 1978-80
Prolific Scottish front man who once scored an unreal nine goals in a single game for The Cherries!

SUPER STAR

Nathan Ake 2017-
Cool, calm, classy and versatile Dutch defender who joined from Chelsea for £20m after a loan spell!

WONDER KID

Lewis Cook Age: 21
The complete midfielder – he can pass, tackle and pulls the strings!

BRIGHTON

LEGEND

Bobby Zamora
2000–03 & 2015–16
Classic No.9 known for his hold-up play and his goal poaching!

SUPER STAR

Lewis Dunk 2010-
This slick ball-playing centre-back has racked up over 200 games since joining as a schoolboy!

WONDER KID

Max Sanders Age: 19
Neat and tidy England Under-19 midfielder, who has quick feet and can dictate the match tempo!

BURNLEY

Jimmy McIlroy
LEGEND
1950–63
Creative midfielder, capped 55 times by Northern Ireland and known as the Brain Of Burnley!

Steven Defour
SUPER STAR
2016-
The Belgium international is a smart midfielder who joined from Anderlecht for a record fee of £8m!

Dwight McNeil
WONDER KID
Age: 18
Skilful attacking midfielder, who joined The Clarets' youth academy from Man. United in 2014!

CARDIFF

Robert Earnshaw
LEGEND
1998-2004 & 2011-13
Wales striker who could conjure up moments of brilliance!

Aron Gunnarsson
SUPER STAR
2011-
Nails Iceland midfielder with a never-say-die attitude who is now in his eighth season with The Bluebirds!

James Waite
WONDER KID
Age: 19
Welsh attacking midfielder who is blessed with great technique and a locker-load of tricks!

CHELSEA

LEGEND

Gianfranco Zola
1996–2003
Gloriously gifted Italian No.10 who could assist, entertain and score unbelievable goals!

SUPER STAR

Eden Hazard 2012-
World-class superstar winger, expert dribbler and three-time Chelsea Player of the Year!

WONDER KID

Callum Hudson-Odoi Age: 17
England Under-17 attacker with pace, a cool head and tekkers for days!

CRYSTAL PALACE

Ian Wright
LEGEND
1985–91
Thrilling, confident and unstoppable English striker who scored lots of spectacular goals for The Eagles!

SUPER STAR

Wilfried Zaha
2010-13 & 2015-
Skilful, speedy and powerful winger!

WONDER KID

Nya Kirby Age: 18
Clever midfielder who won the 2017 Under-17 World Cup with England!

TURN OVER FOR MORE!

EVERTON

FULHAM

HUDDERSFIELD

LEGEND

Dixie Dean
1925–37
Record-breaking powerful English striker who famously scored 60 goals in one season!

SUPER STAR

Jordan Pickford
2017-
England's No.1 – a confident, agile shot-stopper and the most expensive British keeper ever!

WONDER KID

Morgan Feeney
Age: 19
Talented centre-back who's tough in the tackle and strong in the air!

LEGEND

Johnny Haynes
1952–70
Classy playmaker known for his incredible range of passing!

SUPER STAR

Tom Cairney 2015-
Creative left-footed Scotland international midfielder and regular scorer of unstoppable goals!

WONDER KID

Ryan Sessegnon
Age: 18
The rapid left-sided Londoner already is close to 100 senior appearances!

Ray Wilson
1952-64
LEGEND

Attack-minded left-back who was a key part of England's 1966 World Cup-winning team!

SUPER STAR

Aaron Mooy 2016-
All-round Australian midfielder – a pin-point passer and scorer of long-range screamers!

WONDER KID

Matty Daly Age: 17
Talented and creative English midfielder who can cause havoc out wide or centrally as a No.10!

LEICESTER

Gary Lineker
1978–85
Legendary and prolific England striker who started at The Foxes and was a penalty-box predator!

LEGEND

Jamie Vardy 2012-
Energetic all-action striker whose drive, pace and hard work causes defences all sorts of problems!

SUPER STAR

Harvey Barnes
Age: 20
Exciting English attacking mid with quick feet who is a real goal threat!

WONDER KID

LIVERPOOL

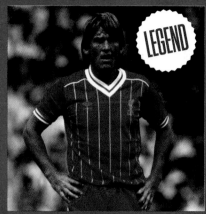

LEGEND

Kenny Dalglish
1977–90
This Scotland forward was known for his touch, creativity and tekkers – a legend for both club and country!

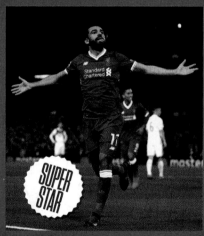

SUPER STAR

Mo Salah 2017-
The turbo-charged Egypt forward was Premier League top scorer and Player of the Year last season!

WONDER KID

Rhian Brewster
Age: 18
Deadly goalscorer and 2017 Under-17 World Cup Golden Boot winner!

MAN. CITY

Colin Bell
1966–79

LEGEND

Quick-footed skilful English midfielder and known as the King of the Kippax!

SUPER STAR

Kevin De Bruyne 2015-
World-class playmaker with unreal technique, unrivalled passing and a rocket shot keepers can't stop!

WONDER KID

Phil Foden Age: 18
English midfielder with close control, an ace touch and amazing balance!

TURN OVER FOR MORE!

MAN. UNITED

LEGEND

George Best
1963–74
Unstoppable dribbling genius from Northern Ireland who had to be seen to be believed!

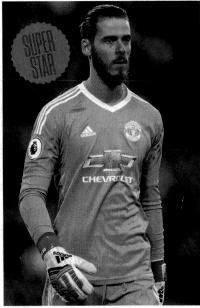

SUPER STAR

David De Gea 2011-
The Spain shot-stopper has amazing reflexes and agility – he's now the best keeper in the world!

WONDER KID

Angel Gomes
Age: 18
Seriously skilful midfielder – he has creativity, composure and sick tricks!

NEWCASTLE

LEGEND

Alan Shearer
1996-2006
Powerful English No.9 who was a record-shattering beast of a striker!

SUPER STAR

Jonjo Shelvey 2016-
This tough-tackling central midfielder loves to get stuck in and spray long cross-field passes!

WONDER KID

Sean Longstaff
Age: 20
Hard-working all-action, goal-scoring midfielder – and a hometown lad!

SOUTHAMPTON

LEGEND

Matt Le Tissier
1986–2002
Laidback English forward who, playing as a No.10, conjured up moments of pure footy genuis!

SUPER STAR

Ryan Bertrand
2015-
UCL-winning left-back who is solid in defence and dangerous in attack!

WONDER KID

Jake Vokins
Age: 18
The England U-18 ace is good on the ball and puts in pinpoint crosses!

TOTTENHAM

LEGEND

Danny Blanchflower
1954–64

The Northern Irish playmaker pulled all the strings in midfield and was at the centre of the action!

SUPER STAR

Harry Kane 2009-

The ultimate striker – Haz is calm, clinical and netted almost 140 goals over the last four seasons!

WONDER KID

Oliver Skipp
Age: 18

Classy English midfielder with great technique and a big passing range!

WATFORD

LEGEND

John Barnes
1981–87

Skillful, entertaining and supremely powerful England left-winger!

SUPER STAR

Abdoulaye Doucoure 2017-

Dynamic midfielder who breaks up attacks before bursting forward!

WONDER KID

Cucho Hernandez
Age: 19

Highly rated Colombia forward who's on loan at La Liga club Huesca!

WEST HAM

LEGEND

Bobby Moore
1958–74

A stylish and cultured centre-back who captained England to World Cup glory back in 1966!

Marko Arnautovic
2017-

SUPER STAR

Tall, skilful and strong Austria frontman who has great technique, super control and a blistering shot!

Declan Rice
Age: 19

WONDER KID

Composed and versatile centre-back and holding midfielder who is two-footed and strong in the air!

WOLVES

Billy Wright
1939–59

LEGEND

Inspirational England centre-back who picked up 105 caps and was known for his reading of the game!

Ruben Neves
2017-

SUPER STAR

Playmaking Portuguese midfielder capable of thumping long-range goals and glorious assists!

WONDER KID

Morgan Gibbs-White
Age: 18

Exciting English attacking midfielder whose movement and pace causes panic in defences!

THE BIG 5!

How do Europe's superclubs compare to each other?

CLUB	COUNTRY	FOUNDED	STADIUM	LEAGUE TITLES
		1902	Santiago Bernabeu 81,044	33
		1899	Nou Camp 99,354	25
		1900	Allianz Arena 75,000	28
		1897	Allianz Stadium 41,507	34
		1970	Parc Des Princes 47,929	7

UCL WINNERS	RECORD SIGNING	MOST APPEARANCES	RECORD SCORER	2018-19 SEASON
13	**GARETH BALE** **£85m** from Tottenham, 2013	**RAUL** **741** GAMES 1994-2010	**CRISTIANO RONALDO** **451** GOALS 2009-18	Manager: Julen Lopetegui Captain: Sergio Ramos Star player: Luka Modric
5	**PHILIPPE COUTINHO** **£142m** from Liverpool, 2018	**XAVI** **767** GAMES 1998-2015	**LIONEL MESSI** **556*** GOALS 2005-	Manager: Ernesto Valverde Captain: Lionel Messi Star player: Lionel Messi
5	**CORENTIN TOLISSO** **£35m** from Lyon, 2017	**SEPP MAIER** **599** GAMES 1962-80	**GERD MULLER** **564** GOALS 1964-79	Manager: Niko Kovac Captain: Manuel Neuer Star player: Robert Lewandowski
2	**CRISTIANO RONALDO** **£99.2m** from Real Madrid, 2018	**ALESSANDRO DEL PIERO** **705** GAMES 1993-2012	**ALESSANDRO DEL PIERO** **290** GOALS 1993-2012	Manager: Massimiliano Allegri Captain: Giorgio Chiellini Star player: Cristiano Ronaldo
0	**NEYMAR** **£198m** from Barcelona, 2017	**JEAN-MARC PILORGET** **445** GAMES 1975-89	**EDINSON CAVANI** **172*** GOALS 2013-	Manager: Thomas Tuchel Captain: Thiago Silva Star player: Kylian Mbappe

All stats correct up to 4 September 2018

MATCH of the DAY
magazine
MOHAMED SALAH
Illustrator: David Diehl
daviddiehl.ch

Cut out & keep your fave posters!

THE ALTERNATIVE
WORLD CUPS OF FOOTBALL!

It's time to end all the arguments. It's your chance to decide – once and for all – just what are the best things in this big incredible world of football!

THIS IS FOOTBALL!

WHAT YOU NEED TO DO:

- We've drawn each first round at random – the rest is up to you!
- Decide who wins each match-up, the winner goes through to the next round and sets up another match-up!
- Continue until you have ONE team left – this is officially the winner!

TURN OVER FOR MORE!

Old Trafford ✗
Goodison Park ✗
— *old Trafford*

Etihad Stadium ✗
Stamford Bridge ✗
— *Stamford bri*

— *Old trafford*

St James' Park ✗
Emirates Stadium ✗
— *St James park*

London Stadium ✗
Hampden Park ✗
— *Emirates*

— *Emirates*

Anfield ✗
Tottenham Stadium ✗
— *King power*

King Power Stadium ✗
Millennium Stadium ✗
— *Tott*

— *old trafford*
— *Tottenham*

Wembley Stadium ✗
Celtic Park ✗
— *Wembley*

Ibrox Stadium ✗
Villa Park ✗
— *Villa*

— *Tottoham*
— *Villa*

WINNER!
— *Old traf*

THE WORLD CUP OF... SPORTS BRANDS!

Which is the best brand in the world? You decide!

Puma ✗
Under Armour ✗
— *Nike*

Nike ✗
Umbro ✗
— *Umbro*

PUMA | UNDER ARMOUR | NIKE | umbro

Reebok ✗
New Balance ✗
— *Hummle*

Hummel ✗
Adidas ✗
— *Adidas*

— *Nike*
— *Adidas*

WINNER!
— *Adidas*

Reebok ▲ | new balance | hummel | adidas

THE WORLD CUP OF... WONDERGOALS!

What is the best type of goal you can score? You decide!

Overhead kick	✗			
Thumping volley	✗	*overhead*		
Curling free-kick	✗	*Slik cou*	*Overheed*	
Slick counter-attack	✗		*solo run*	**WINNER!** *Overhead*
30-yard screamer	✗			
Diving header	✗	*solo run*		
Solo run	✗	*Diving*		
Cheeky chip	✗			

THE WORLD CUP OF... FOOTY MANAGERS!

Who is the best manager in the world? You decide!

Gareth Southgate	✗			
Unai Emery	✗	*Gareth*		
Massimiliano Allegri	✗	*Emery*	*Gareth*	
Carlo Ancelotti	✗		*Carlo*	
Antonio Conte	✗			
Jurgen Klopp	✗	*Conte*		
Roberto Martinez	✗	*klopp*		*Gareth*
Pep Guardiola	✗			*Diego*
Niko Kovac	✗			
Diego Simeone	✗	*Pochettino*		
Mauricio Pochettino	✗	*Diego*		
Didier Deschamps	✗		*Zide*	
Zinedine Zidane	✗		*Diego*	
Maurizio Sarri	✗	*Zidne*		
Thomas Tuchel	✗	*Mourny*		
Jose Mourinho	✗			

WINNER! *Gareth*

TURN OVER FOR MORE!

THE WORLD CUP OF... FOOTY LEGENDS!

Who is the best player of all time? You decide!

- Diego Maradona ✗
- Alfredo Di Stefano ✗ → D. MARADONA
- Johan Cruyff ✗ → L. MESSI
- Lionel Messi ✗
- Cristiano Ronaldo ✗
- Franz Beckenbauer ✗ → C. RONALDO
- Pele ✗ → Z. ZIDANE
- Zinedine Zidane ✗

L. MESSI
C. RONALDO

C. RONALDO

WINNER!

THE WORLD CUP OF... SUPERCLUBS!

Which of these is the biggest club in the world? You decide!

- Man. United ✗
- Atletico Madrid ✗ → Man City
- Man. City ✗ → PSG
- PSG ✗
- Arsenal ✗
- Barcelona ✗ → PSG
- Liverpool ✗ → Barcelona
- Roma ✗
- Borussia Dortmund
- Juventus ✗ → PSG
- Inter Milan ✗ → inter
- Bayern Munich ✗
- AC Milan
- Tottenham ✗ → PSG
- Chelsea ✗ → AC Milan
- Real Madrid ✗

PSG
Borussia Dortmund

PSG
BVB

PSG
Man. C

WINNER!
PSG

THE WORLD CUP OF... HALF-TIME FOOD!

What's the best snack for fans? You decide!

Steak & kidney pie	✗			
Salt & vinegar crisps	✗	*pie*		
Sausage roll	✗	*crisp*	*crisp*	
Banana	✗		*pizza*	
Oreos	✗			
Chicken pie	✗	*pizza*		
Pizza slice	✗	*Mars bar*		*pizza*
Mars bar	✗			*burger*
Hot dog	✗			
Cheese & onion crisps	✗	*Hotdog*		
Bacon roll	✗	*Burger*		
Burger	✗		*Burger*	
Cornish Pasty	✗		*chips*	
Chips	✗	*pasty*		
Ham sandwich	✗	*chips*		
Tomato soup	✗			

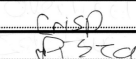

WINNER!

Pizza

THE WORLD CUP OF... COMPETITIONS!

Which is the best footy comp in the world? You decide!

Premier League	✗	*Prem Prem*	
Ligue 1	✗	*UP Champ*	
Champions League	✗		*champ world*
Bundesliga	✗		*world cup*
La Liga	✗		
FA Cup	✗	*La*	
Serie A	✗	*camp world*	
World Cup	✗		

BUNDESLIGA

WINNER!

QUIZ ANSWERS!

How well did you do? Check your scores below quizzers...

Where you from, mate?
1 B 2 C 3 A 4 B 5 A
6 B 7 A 8 B 9 A

MY SCORE [ANSWER] OUT OF 9

A year in football!
1 A 2 A 3 C 4 C 5 A
6 C 7 B 8 B 9 A

MY SCORE [ANSWER] OUT OF 9

Stadium name game!
1 B 2 C 3 A 4 A 5 B
6 C 7 B 8 B 9 A

MY SCORE [ANSWER] OUT OF 9

Family footy quiz!
English football:
1 A 2 A 3 C 4 A 5 B
6 C 7 B 8 D 9 B 10 A

MY SCORE [ANSWER] OUT OF 10

Rest of the world:
11 D 12 C 13 B 14 B 15 B
16 C 17 B 18 C 19 A 20 C

MY SCORE [ANSWER] OUT OF 20

CHAMPION Did you ace our quizzes? Thought so – legend!

MATCH of the DAY

Write to us at...

Match of the Day magazine
Immediate Media, Vineyard House,
44 Brook Green, Hammersmith,
London, W6 7BT

Telephone 020 7150 5513

Email shout@motdmag.com
pazandketch@motdmag.com
motdmag.com

Match Of The Day editor	Ian Foster	Production editor	Neil Queen-Jones
Annual editor	Mark Parry	Deputy production editor	Joe Shackley
Senior art editor	Blue Buxton	Publishing consultant	Jaynie Bye
Designer	Pete Rogers	Editorial director	Corinna Shaffer
Digital editor/senior writer	Matthew Ketchell	Annual images	Getty Images
Features editor	Lee Stobbs		
Group picture editor	Natasha Thompson		
Picture editor	Jason Timson		

BBC Books an imprint of Ebury Publishing 20 Vauxhall Bridge Road London SW1V 2SA. BBC Books is part of the Penguin Random House group of companies whose addresses can be found at global.penguinrandomhouse.com. Copyright © Match Of The Day magazine 2018. First published by BBC Books in 2018 www.penguin.co.uk. A CIP catalogue record for this book is available from the British Library. ISBN 9781785942051. Commissioning editor: Albert DePetrillo; project editor: Benjamin McConnell; production: Phil Spencer. Printed and bound in Italy by Rotolito Lombarda SpA. Penguin Random House is committed to a sustainable future for our business our readers and our planet. This book is made from Forest Stewardship Council ® certified paper.

BBC

The licence to publish this magazine was acquired from BBC Studios by Immediate Media Company on 1 November 2011. We remain committed to making a magazine of the highest editorial quality one that complies with BBC editorial and commercial guidelines and connects with BBC programmes.

Match Of The Day Magazine is is published by Immediate Media Company London Limited under licence from BBC Studios. © Immediate Media Company London Limited 2018.

DON'T EXPECT ME TO PUT THE BINS OUT ON A TUESDAY!

I'M TOO BUSY READING...

MATCH of the DAY magazine

GET YOUR MOTD MAG FIX EVERY WEEK!*

*bin bags not included

MY PREDICTIONS FOR 2018-19!

YOUR FACT FILE!

STICK A PHOTO OF YOURSELF HERE!

NAME: I dont wanna tell me name   **AGE:** 8/10

HOMETOWN: London dah

FAVOURITE TEAM: why are u so PSG/Mancity England

FAVOURITE PLAYER: Nemare Personel?

Q1 WHO WILL WIN THE PREMIER LEAGUE?
The final Premier League match of the season is on Sunday 12 May – so who will be celebrating?

Man cit

2017-18: MAN. CITY

Q2 WHO WILL WIN THE PREM GOLDEN BOOT?
Mohamed Salah's 32 goals last term were the most scored by anyone in a 38-game Prem season!

Mo salah

2017-18: MOHAMED SALAH

Q3 WHO WILL BE PFA PLAYER OF THE YEAR?
This is the award voted for by all Prem players – it's the players' very own hero of the season!

Nemare

2017-18: MOHAMED SALAH

PAZ SAYS
There are so many contenders this season – Salah, De Bruyne, Hazard, Auba. What a league!